SUFFICIENT Grace FOR THE JOURNEY

How a Carolina Tomboy Became a Woman of God

MELISSA HALSTEAD

Sufficient Grace for the Journey Paperback
Copyright © 2025 Melissa Halstead
ALL RIGHTS RESERVED WORLDWIDE

ISBN: 978-1-951280-54-3

Unless otherwise noted, Scriptures are taken from the KING JAMES VERSION®. Public Domain.

Cover Design: Don Patton Creative

DEDICATION

This book is dedicated to Jesus, for giving me the strength and courage to finish my journey. To God be the glory!

ACKNOWLEDGEMENTS

A special thank you to my spouse, who endured late nights and countless revisions with me, and a smile to my daughter, who encouraged me for many years to write a book.

TABLE OF CONTENTS

i	Introduction	1
1	Chapter One	6
2	Chapter Two	10
3	Chapter Three	24
4	Chapter Four	33
5	Chapter Five	37
6	Chapter Six	41
7	Chapter Seven	53
8	Chapter Eight	62
9	Chapter Nine	67
10	Chapter Ten	82
11	Chapter Eleven	85
12	Chapter Twelve	94

INTRODUCTION

I will be the first to tell you how unworthy I am to write this book. But God's words are so worthy to be heard. Without Him I am nothing.

While I was laying in my bed praying about writing this book, I said, "God help me to write what we all need to hear and understand. Help me to be one of Your servants to Your word and help me to say only what You would have me to say." He responded, "Explain to others who are saved by My grace that they are only passing through this world to a better world."

We are not to get distraught and burdened down with the things of this world because it is not our home. You are only here as a witness and servant for God. You will never feel fully at home in this world because you don't belong here. We have all sinned and will continue to sin as long as we are here in this world, because this world is a sinful place that Satan has corrupted. This is no excuse, this is truth. This world is corrupt, violent, angry, and hostile toward the things of God and if you choose to follow God, the devils of this world will try to kill you. They want your soul, your mind, and your spirit.

The difference between the saved and the unsaved is that the saved choose to walk with Christ, to believe in Him and His word. We choose to study Him through His word, and we know and believe that He took our sins to the cross with Him and died in our place. The unsaved choose not to believe in Him or that He came and took their sins with Him to the cross. Some even believe if they are good enough by being good to others and taking care of "mother earth" that their reward is Heaven when they die. This is a lie the devil has told them, and one they choose to believe.

As Jesus said to Moses in Exodus 3:14, "And GOD said unto Moses, I AM THAT I AM," He also says to us in John 14:6, "Jesus answered, 'I am the way, the truth, and the life. No one comes to the Father, but by me.'" You can only be saved by believing in Jesus Christ. There is no other way!! You must believe for yourself and demonstrate your faith by the way you live your life. As James 2:26 says, "For as the body without the spirit is dead, so faith without works is dead also."

Think back to when you were a child and the belief you had in Santa Claus. No matter what anyone told you, you still believed there was a Santa Clause. This is the simple, child-like faith God wants you to have in Jesus Christ and what He did for you on the cross. Believe that He is real, and believe that He came just to save you because He loves you. He is pleased with us just because we believed in Him. John 6:28-29 says, "Then said they into him, 'What shall we do, that we might work the works of God?' Jesus answered and said unto them, 'This is the work of God that ye believe on him whom he hath sent.'" The one thing that is required of you is that you believe in the one whom God has sent. This is the first step of your journey, where it all begins by taking the first step toward Christ.

I'm so thankful He doesn't say clean yourself up and get your house in order then I will save you. He says come as you are right now. You may be in a state of confusion, you may be hurt, angry, or even broken, you may feel like no one loves you or ever will love you, but Christ is saying to you, "Come to me, come as you are, let me help you, let me love you, I can fix the brokenness you feel and put you back together with a love you have never known." He is saying to you, "I can take away the confusion and anger and replace it with the peace and joy in your soul. I will replace the hurt you feel with happiness and love."

You have one job to do to come to Him and believe that He can do what He says He will do. Most people will not do this, partly because of pride, partly because we often feel that we are too broken for anyone to fix, and partly because we have always had to do things on our own and therefore, we don't trust anyone to fix it for us. We overlook the fact He is God and not man. He will not fail us the way that people have.

Personally, I was the one no one could fix. In my mind, I had made the mess in my life, and I was supposed to fix it. I was supposed to clean it up. I remember one time going to my grandma's as a young woman, I still called her Granny. At the time, my husband was abusing me and I had two young children at home. I never told her that my husband was abusive, I just told her that I needed a place to stay for a little while. Her response back to me was, "You made your bed; you lay in it." I was deeply hurt by those words for a long time, but I understood what she was saying. She was saying, "Don't give up just because things seem hard, you can make it work." If I could go back now and talk to myself then, I would tell myself, "When going through difficult times, give it to God. He will see you through, He will make thigs work for your good and His Glory."

Let me just say here, abuse is never acceptable, but you must be honest with people when and if you need help. You must tell them the whole truth. I didn't tell my granny the whole story, so she just thought I was having normal marital issues and wanted to quit, to give up. She didn't have all the details, and I was too ashamed and embarrassed to tell her everything that was happening to me. I was also too prideful to admit that she was right, I was too young for marriage and motherhood, and too stubborn to listen to her godly wisdom.

One of the best things about serving the LORD is that He already knows and sees *all* that is happening to you, and He can fix it when you cry out to Him. Pray for the LORD to show you where to go and what to do next. He will open doors for you and if the door closes, then He will open a window. He will always make a way for you. My granny was a God-fearing woman who loved the LORD and always tried her best to do what His word says. There was always a peace about her because of her walk with the LORD. I felt this peace from her and craved it in my life but in my youth, I didn't understand that the peace she had was coming from her walk with the LORD.

My hope and prayer is that by reading this book, you will be stirred in your heart to want the peace that my granny had and that thankfully, I now also have because I am fully walking with Christ. I will share with you my story and how God rescued me from myself, the one no one else could fix…but Christ could, and He did. I want the same for you.

CHAPTER ONE

My grandma, which is to say my mom's mother, died when I was 6, almost 7. It was June. I had seen my grandma in a dream, in Heaven. She was dying of cancer in her bed at her home. She had taken a turn for the worse, and they called my mom to drive her to the hospital. Of course, I had to go with my mom. They placed my grandma in the back seat of my mom's car. On our way to the hospital, I was looking over the front seat into the back seat, I remember Grandma throwing up on the way to the hospital.

That night was when I had the dream. I dreamed that Grandma was in Heaven. She was standing on the other side of the small river. I looked down at the river and it was crystal clear. I could see all the small smooth rocks in my dream, and the water looked to be about 10 feet wide. She was wearing a white flowing gown. I could see beautiful flowers everywhere, of all colors. Colors I didn't know and had never seen before. There were rocks piled on each side of a small waterfall on my right. Grandma was standing directly across the water from me with her arms opened wide, smiling. She was in a field of flowing grass. She would open her arms like this when we would go visit. She would say, "Don't let the screen door slam!" as we would come running through the back door and down the hall of the old house. She always seemed to be standing in the kitchen. The door to the kitchen was on the left just down the hall and it was always open. Grandma would always hold her arms open wide, and I would wrap my arms around her waist as she wrapped her arms completely around me with a hug. That very same night that I had this dream, she died at the hospital.

A few days later when we were at her graveside, I couldn't cry because I kept seeing her across from me at the river. She wasn't sick or throwing up, she was happy with a huge smile on her face, and her arms were open wide waiting to hug us. How could I cry over that? Several of my family members said to me, "Why are you not crying?" That was when I told everyone about my dream. I don't know if they believed me then, but I know they will see her when they reach Heaven.

In my life, this is how I have pictured Christ. He is standing with his arms open wide saying, "Come to me, join me in Heaven, let me hold you, let me comfort you, let me help you." He is constantly standing there waiting and calling for anyone and everyone who will only believe in Him. He is there at the door, as Revelation 3:20-21 says, "Behold I stand at the door, and knock: if any man hear my voice, and open the door, I will come into him, and will sup with him, he with me. To him that overcometh will I grant to sit with me in my throne, even as I also overcame, and am set down with my Father in His throne."

The LORD is saying to us, "I stand at your heart's door and knock. If you will open your heart's door by believing in me, I will come into your heart to live with you." When you have finished the work I have for you here on this earth, then you will come into Heaven and sit with Jesus in His seat. I picture this as sitting in an oversized chair waiting for my children or grandchildren to come visit. When they come into my home, which is their home, I want them to come right over and sit down with me so I can hold them, speak with them and especially, so I can love on them.

This is how your Father in Heaven feels about you. He loves you. If you want to know Him and what He can do for you or in your life, you must spend time with Him. Like any relationship, whatever time you put into it dictates how much it grows. Similar to a plant in a garden, if you want it to grow you must feed it, talk to it, and water it. This is what you must do with your relationship with Christ. You must spend the time to get to know Him by reading His word, listening to music that glorifies Him, talking to Him, listening for Him to talk to you, and talking to others about Him. If you want the relationship to die, then just sit on the church pew, act like you are listening and go back out and do nothing. This is rejecting God's offer to have a relationship with you. You are starving your spiritual soul, and it will surely die. It is this simple.

CHAPTER TWO

I remember it plain as day. It was 1978 and I was in the VBS, Vacation Bible School at Gordon Baptist, with Granny. We were reading John Chapter 9 that week. Each child was taking a turn reading a verse. I quickly read on ahead to see what was going to be my verse because I wanted to make sure that I would say each word correctly. I didn't want to get laughed at and sometimes, the words are hard to pronounce. I was to read verse 11, "He answered and said, a man that is called Jesus made clay, and anointed mine eyes, and said unto me, 'Go to the pool of Siloam, and wash' and I went, and I washed, and I received sight."

This verse hit me like a lightning bolt. I knew within my soul that if I would believe and do what Jesus said, then I would be healed and made to see Him. I so desperately wanted to know Him. I wanted to know He was real, not just someone you read about who can do miracles. I truly enjoyed going to church and at that very minute, He became real to me, not just a story in a book.

I felt like I was the blind man in the Bible. The teacher had us do an exercise to understand what it was like to be blind. She had us all cup our hands over our eyes and try to walk around for 5 minutes in the room. Then she said, "This is how it is when Christ doesn't live in you. When you are not saved you are blind. You wander around in the darkness, you stumble, and you fall, and there is no one there to help you up. You get hurt and no one cares. Then one day Jesus the Holy Spirit comes to you and says, 'Do you want to see?' and you answer yes, or you answer no to Him." The teacher then said, "Would you answer yes or no?" and of course we all said, "Yes! We want to see!"

The Teacher then said, "Sit down at the table." Our eyes were still shut. The teacher said, "I have placed a bowl of water in front of you. If you want to see, take your hands from your eyes, scoop up the water in each hand, and wash away the darkness." She explained to us that the darkness was from sin in our lives and the water was the blood that was shed from Christ as He suffered and died on the cross. She told us that everyone makes their own choice to be blind and live in sin, or to see by being saved through the blood of Jesus. She said, "The sin made you blind, but believing in Christ makes you see the truth." I understood that I needed to ask Christ to come live in my soul and body. As a nine-year-old child, I understood this. I knew if I believed in

Christ, I would see Him one day and I could be with my grandma in Heaven when I died. This was a place I had heard Granny, Grandma, and my aunt talk about many times. I was anxious to go there. I was searching for peace.

In your life, once you come to believe in Christ and you choose to follow Him, you are one of His children and you are instantly on your way to Heaven. This means that when you become saved you are already seated with Christ in Heaven. Your physical body is still here on earth, but your spirit is with the LORD in Heaven. When your body dies here on earth, your spirit does not die but remains with the LORD in Heaven.

When you believe in Jesus, your sins are covered with the blood that He shed, and you are forgiven. Your sins are cast as far away as the east is from the west, and He remembers them no more. (See Psalm 103:12, Hebrews 8:12.) Every time you think of your sin, which the devil will try to remind you of often, remind the devil that God remembers it no more, and that Jesus paid for all of your sins on the cross. The person you used to be is still living in this world and wants to draw you back to a sin nature. This is what we refer to as the old man. Because of this old man, you will sin again or have bad thoughts. You must fight him by getting closer and closer to God.

Remember that being saved is not a get out of jail free card. You can't deliberately or defiantly sin. It is not a free ticket to do what you want and then ask for God's forgiveness. When you are truly saved, you will want to do what is right. You will want to get closer to God. You will want to please Him and do what you know is right by God's commandments. You will want to do what is holy and when you do wrong, you should feel the Holy Spirit within you nudging you that it's not right and to fix it. This means that you must humble yourself and do whatever you can to fix the wrong you have done, the sin you have just committed.

If you do not feel that nudge within you from the Holy Spirit to fix what you have done when you have done wrong, then you are not saved. When you become saved, Christ comes to live in you. He can't dwell in the unsaved and doesn't dwell in the lost. That is why when you are saved but you do something wrong, you hear God's voice or what some call a prick in your spirit that says, "You know that this is wrong, so go and make it right." He will not let you get by with doing wrong, He loves you too much.

There will be times when we do not know how to fix the problem we have created or that others have created for us. In these times, it is most important to be quiet, to be still, and *not* to take matters into our own hands. We will mess it up. But if we just hold our ground, pray to God, and trust that He will answer, He will make a way out for us.

You are His child. He, as your Father, will always be there to help you in times of need. Remember God's timing is not always your timing, but He will not forget about your problem. In your difficulties and trials, God is teaching you to trust Him more. How you handle the situation determines how much you grow in Christ.

When we don't trust that it is all about believing God and His word, I think this is because in our mind, it seems too simple. So, we add to the process of salvation, and we complicate things. The devil's job is to confuse people's minds. As Proverbs 23:7 says about an enemy, "For as he thinketh in his heart, so is he: Eat and drink, saith he to thee; but his heart is not with thee." Where is your heart? If it is with Christ, your mind is on the things of Christ but if your mind is on the things of the world, then that is where your heart is.

In our mind it is extremely hard to trust in the plan of salvation, something so simple. We have this attitude from phrases we have been taught from others in our life. Phrases like, "if it is too good to be true, it must not be true," and "if it is that easy, something is wrong with it." This is a complex worldview.

When you invite Christ into your soul and life, you start to trust Him little by little, as is true in other relationships. Trials come, and you learn to lean on Christ and His word to help you through them. This is how your faith grows and you learn to trust Him more and more.

The more you trust Him, the more you share with Him. This process is harder for some than others because of past hurts from people we trusted. But, we must remind ourselves that Christ is not like others. He doesn't judge us from our past mistakes and failures. As Isaiah 61:7 says, "For your shame ye shall have double, and for your confusion they shall rejoice in their portion: therefore in their land they shall possess the double: everlasting joy shall be unto them." This is Christ saying to His children, "For your shame and confusion you shall receive everlasting joy." He is always on our side. He loves us right where we are. He desires a close intimate walk with us. He will get as close to you as you will let Him, but He will not force you to come to Him.

When you begin your walk with Christ, there will still be many times you will ask yourself why didn't I just believe and come to know Him sooner? He waits to hear from you. Every little detail of your life is precious to Him. He longs to hear from His children in the big stuff, small stuff, all stuff, important or not, He wants to hear it from you.

It is hard for some to believe that God could love them this much. It is because we know all of the bad things we have done and all of the wrong thoughts we have thought. We compare God to our own human father here on earth, but the truth is that He is not human; He is God, the creator of all things, and He won't fail. Numbers 23:19 says, "God is not a man, that he should lie; neither the son of man, that he should repent: hath he said, and shall he not do it? or hath he spoken, and shall not make it good?"

God wants to bless you, and He wants to help you. Numbers 23:20 says, "Behold I have received commandment to bless: and he hath blessed; and I cannot reverse it." This journey you and I are on is not an easy walk, but I believe the LORD's promises to be true, and I know in the end it will be worth every step.

You may feel like you are alone, but God said He will never leave you or forsake you. When you feel all alone, you are being tested. This is building your trust and your faith. This is teaching you patience because with patience you bear fruit. Bearing fruit means others are seeing you walk with Christ and will hopefully make the decision to follow Him. Others grow strong in their belief of Christ because of what they see you going through and how you handle it.

Ask yourself: Do the people around me see me walking with Christ or do they see me walking with the world? Do they see me falling apart, or giving it all to Christ? Do they see me obeying His commandments and His word, or do they see me becoming overwhelmed and angry with God?

Matthew 5 is a wonderful chapter that everyone should take time to study. We can read it devotionally and ask ourselves: Do others see me as hungry for Christ or do they see me as hungry for the things of this world? Does Christ see me as having a merciful pure heart as a peacemaker? Do others see me following Christ, honoring, and obeying Him above all?

You never know who is watching you. It could be your children or grandchildren, your friends or coworkers, or even your parents or your grandparents. If Christ lives in you, then let Him shine through you. He is not to be hidden but lifted high above all. He will give you the words you need to express yourself so that others will see Him in you. His guidance will never lead you wrong. But first, you have to trust Him, and trust him with all you have. You must know He is your all in all, and that only through Him are you made sure.

Romans 12:2 says, "And be not conformed to this world: but be ye transformed by the renewing of your mind, that ye may prove what is that good, and acceptable, and perfect, will of God." You must renew your mind; you can do this by studying on the things of God. 2 Corinthians 10:5 says, "Casting down imaginations, and every high thing that exalteth itself against the knowledge of God, and bringing into captivity every thought to the obedience of Christ." When you have wrong thoughts, you can control them by casting them down and thinking of good and godly things instead. Set your mind and keep it set on the LORD and things above. Say to yourself, "He loves me right here just as I am. Repeat, He loves me." Say this as many times as you need to daily to yourself.

When you have sinned, ask Him for forgiveness and then trust that He has forgiven you. You must let it go and continue your journey with Christ. The LORD doesn't bring it back to memory, the devil does. The devil wants you to spend your time getting upset and regretting the past sin in your life so you will not go on for Christ. When the devil attacks you, say to him, "I am the righteousness of Christ, He has cast my sin away as far as the east is from the west and He remembers it no more. I am a child of the King." Then, straighten your crown, put on your armor of God, and get back to walking with Christ.

Reading the Bible, God's holy word, we see battle after battle. This is what we do as Christians. Today, we live in a world that is offended by everyone and everything, and we fight battle after battle. Sometimes, it is on the outside with worldly things like acceptance of abortion, people killing others, wars we don't understand, violence, or abuse of others where no one seems to be punished, or a government that has turned its back on the people and what we stand for. Other times, the battle is within us, feelings we can't seem to overcome like depression, anger, hurt, worry, anxiety, feeling like we are doing all we can but can never get ahead. During all of these battles the LORD is watching and waiting for you to trust Him. We as humans think those battles are for us to fight but if you are a child of God, then the battle is His, not yours. When we trust Him, He will fight the battle and, however it works out, it will be for our good and His glory.

We are to follow His commandment to love one another as Christ loves us. This is for our good, this is because we can't enter into Heaven with hate in our soul. I don't know what you have seen, but some of the people confessing to be Christians must not understand this commandment or maybe they don't understand that our sins are what nailed Christ to a cross. He loved us anyway. When we refuse to love and forgive, we are bearing no fruit for Christ. In the Book of Revelation, Christ warned these people and called them lukewarm. Revelation 3:16: "So then because thou art lukewarm, and neither cold nor hot, I will spew thee out of my mouth." It is time we wake up and show the people around us how good the LORD truly is. He didn't save us just to be with Him in Heaven one day or just to sit on a church bench. He saved us and called us and set us apart to share the gospel with others, so that all who believe will be saved from Hell and will be with Him in glory.

People in the United States of America are growing colder and colder toward God and the things of God. Look at our churches… for those of us who still even attend church. We listen to the word of God, we open the song books, and we might sing loud enough for ourselves to hear, but we're careful not to sing so loud that others hear us because we are too ashamed or worried what others will think of us. I have been guilty of this, too, because I didn't want others to look at me like I was crazy or loud, but can you imagine how that must hurt the LORD? He gave us a voice to hear and hands to raise and worship Him. We are to be rejoicing with uplifting arms and hands, giving praise and worship to Him. He is worthy of all praise and worship. Luke 19:40 says, "And He answered and said unto them, I tell you that, if these should hold their peace, the stones would immediately cry out." In the verse right before this, the Pharisees are saying to rebuke the people who were praising Jesus because the multitude of the disciples were rejoicing and saying blessed be the king. We should be loud, we should be rejoicing to our Father, we should be praising and worshipping because of His goodness. Look at all He has given you, all He has done for you, all He is doing now, and all He has kept you from. He is your savior, your redeemer, your best friend, the one who laid down His life for you. He is the one who will take you from this world one day to a world of peace, where there is no more death, no more departing from people you love, and no more pain. Think about it. We should be singing and rejoicing from the rooftop, singing with a loud voice for others to hear what He has done for us. When you start to worry about what others think and say, just take a look at the cross and all He did just for you, and just for me, and ask yourself if He is worthy of our praise and worship. Your answer to this question will always be yes, He is so worthy. Then, with your voice, with your heart, with your laugh, lift him up so others can see what He has saved you from.

I believe COVID-19 was a wakeup call. I think it was God's way of seeing if we would trust Him or if we would trust man. Whether you took the shot or not, I believe He was watching to see how we treated each other. I have already written about our commandments to love one another but during this test in our lives, many began to hate, to turn against others, to judge others, to banish family members, they began to only care for themselves, and they let fear overrule them.

For some of us it was the beginning of the end of

life; for some, the end of relationships; for others, the end of trust. For a few, it was when you accepted Christ as your savior, so it was the end of your running from God.

John 16:33 says, "These things I have spoken unto you, that in me ye might have peace. In the world ye shall have tribulation; but be of good cheer, I have overcome the world." There were a couple of times during COVID that my flesh wanted to panic and to turn away from everyone, and hide in my little corner of the world, but I kept reminding myself that God is in control of this world; He made it and everything in it; and nothing is going to happen to me that He didn't already know about; and whatever was to happen, He was with me. Only He would be with me to the end.

No man's viruses or anything can keep you from Christ or Him from you. He lives inside you. He is always with His children. Deuteronomy 31:8 says, "And the LORD, He it is that doeth go before thee; He will be with thee, He will not fail thee, neither forsake thee: fear not, neither be dismayed." He is saying to us, "Don't be stressed or worried. I got this. You just trust and rest in my peace." I have no doubt that if the LORD doesn't come soon, we will see more and more tribulations. He is calling to everyone to come to Him. Those who do will know His peace, as Philippians 4:7 says, "And the peace of God, which passes all understanding, shall keep your hearts and minds through Christ Jesus." He is waiting for you; do you know Him?

CHAPTER THREE

We lived with my grandmother, my dad's mom, aka Granny, until I was five years old. She had taken my dad and his brother and moved to a house down the street from my grandfather. My grandfather was abusive to her and their children. He had many women friends, and my granny left him in order to survive. She never married again and to my knowledge, never dated anyone else.

My brother and I were so blessed to come home to a godly Granny that knew how to pray and that loved us as her own. Every Sunday and Wednesday she went to church, and my brother and I would go with her if we were not with our mom. She was always there for us.

Granny made my dad leave when I was two years old and my brother was eight. Daddy drank and when he came home drunk, he was abusive to my mom. Granny was our protector, our safe place. In her home we learned to pray, to go to church, and to respect our elders. I don't remember Daddy and Mom living together at Granny's house as a family.

The first memory I have is riding in the car, laying my head in Mom's lap and being dropped off at my great aunt's house so that Mom and Granny could go to work. While I was there, I ate my aunt's washing powders; it was not good. The next memory I have is going to the nursing home where Granny worked. We got to see where she stayed and sometimes, she rode home in the car with us. That next summer she took me to the swimming pool in town to go swimming. She said I swam like a fish. We worked in the garden that morning and then, we walked to the pool and afterwards, we ate at Ray's Burger King.

The youngest memory I have of my grandfather was looking for rocks in the creek near the hospital in our town. I still have the rock I found that day; it looks like a baby foot. The first memory I have of my stepfather is waiting outside with his son. We were playing on the handrail while my mom and him were being married by the Justice of the Peace. My brother was not there.

My journey started when I was young. As I said before, I have always wanted to go to church. I craved to have the normal family. My dream at this time was that my real dad would come back. In my mind, that would fix all that was wrong with our lives. I wanted the peace I could see in other families. A mom and a dad that didn't yell and scream at each other, no turmoil, only peace.

I was five years old when my mom married my stepfather. I started finding things in our home I had never seen before. Inappropriate things that children should not see. Symbols of vulgar things, nude magazines, nude cards, and even cups that are not for the eyes of children.

My mom and stepdad argued most days. I remember the yelling, cursing, throwing things, and lots of threatening to hurt each other. Of course, Mom threatening to leave him always followed, but she never did, at least not while I was home.

We moved a lot. The most I remember staying in one spot was five years. We moved from a trailer into a brick house, but we were able to stay in the same neighborhood. My mother always made sure we stayed in the same school system, and I am thankful for that. During the day when I was at school, or my brother was home, I knew I was safe, but nighttime was coming and sometimes my brother wasn't going to be there. I would place every stuffed animal and doll I had in the bed with me to cover my head and go to sleep. I prayed most nights that the yelling would stop, and that God would protect my mom, and not let Granny die.

Some nights, I would dream that the wolves were chasing me. In my dream, I just kept running and running. Other nights, it was more normal childhood dreams. My favorite dreams were of flying. I could fly anywhere I wanted around my room, outside to play with my friends and even to a friend's house to play.

There were some days of peace when the house was quiet, and no one hardly spoke. There were also times of joy where Mom would laugh, and it seemed like we could almost be normal. Sometimes, this would last for a few days but then I would come home from school, and she would be in bed sleeping or crying in the closet. I wanted so much to help her; I just didn't know how. I thought that if I was quiet, and all my homework was done, and the house was clean, and my room was clean and organized, then she would be okay. But she wasn't. No matter what I seemed to do, it wasn't enough to help her. My brother was 12 years old and would try to stay busy with friends or baseball outside. Anything to not be in the house.

I would try to go with my stepdad when he would leave. Sometimes, my brother would go too. Those were the best days. We would go with him on the weekends to visit my stepfather's mom and dad for lunch. There were always lots of people there and plenty to do.

His son lived there. He was only 3 years older than me. I would try to follow him and all the other kids to the barn to play. There was an old tire swing hanging from a huge tree in the back yard. It was made from a regular tire with a steel cable attached to it that ran up to the tree limb and around. We spent most of our time outside on that swing, as if we were trying to wear it out.

The days my brother didn't go, my stepdad always had to stop and pee behind a tree but always close enough to where I could see him. All of him. He always drove down a curvy backroad to his parents' house on the way back home and if we were alone, he would ask me if I wanted to drive. He held me on his lap with one hand on my left inner thigh and the other hand near the bottom of the steering wheel. I wasn't tall enough to reach the gas or brake so he would do that for me. Sometimes he would touch me through my shorts or panties. I felt like a big girl because I was driving, and that made me feel special because he wanted to spend time with me. Looking back now, I realize what was happening, but as a child you don't. As a child you just want attention, good or bad; you just want affection, to be wanted.

Momma dreaded the fall and winter. She said it looked like everything was dead or dying. But, she loved Christmas. It was her favorite time of year, and when she put up the Christmas tree, it was as perfect as a picture in a magazine. When we were all home and it would snow, she would go out and sled with us, have snowball fights, and make snow cream.

During the summer and spring, she would play croquet with us and cards at night. She was a kid at heart, and I could tell that these were some of her happiest times. These were the best days for her and for us, but the dark days were always lingering in the background, waiting like death coming. When the dark days came, she was a scared little girl hiding away within herself.

By this time, we had moved at least four times, and Mom was having to drive us to school. For a while, she would drop us at school when it was still dark out. My brother and I would skinny through the chains and padlock on the door of the school building. We would snuggle up to the heater near the library door. We were not the only children there, but we were normally the first ones during the morning. Once the school building opened and the teachers started coming in, my brother would leave to walk down to the middle school. In the afternoon we rode the bus home. When my brother went over to a friend's house after school, I would try to stop at a friend's house on the way home from the bus stop.

My mom wasn't doing well, and she would sleep a lot. My brother called it sleeping with "Prince Valium." I was seven years old and my grandmother, my mom's mom, had passed away a few months earlier. Those were my hardest days because when she was sleeping, and my brother wasn't there, my stepdad would try to lure me to the basement to make me touch him. He would always say he was going to hurt my mom if I didn't do what he said but I thank God that he never raped me, and he didn't kill my mom. I told my mom many times what he was doing. At first, she didn't believe me, so I told my aunt. My aunt believed me, but later in life she told me she didn't do anything because back then, they would have put me in foster care. She was afraid that they would place me somewhere worse than where I already was.

Mom inquired at Department of Social Services about any assistance that might be available if she took us and left my stepdad, but they said that we didn't qualify because we were white, and because she was working. After that, Mom withdrew more and more. She started to look at me like I was her competition. I felt like it was my fault. More and more, I missed my dad. I knew he could fix it, but I would never tell him what my stepdad was doing to me because I was ashamed and because I thought that he wouldn't love me. I swore to myself that when I had children, I would protect them and their father would always be there, no matter the cost.

By this time, I was eight years old and my grandfather, my mom's dad, had come to live with us. They made the basement into his bedroom. I didn't go to the basement anymore. I am not sure how long he lived with us but looking back, it only seemed like just a few weeks.

I came home one day from school and was in my bedroom playing when my grandfather came upstairs. He opened my door and forced me down on the bed. He was starting to pull off my clothes when I got away from him. I ran to my friend's house screaming and crying. I told my friend's mom all that had happened. When I went back home, my uncle, Mom, and stepdad were there, and I could see my grandfather laying in the back of a car. His head was bleeding, I could hear people saying he was drunk, and I could hear my mom saying that he couldn't stay with us anymore. My uncle took my grandfather away with him that day. The next time I saw my grandfather was when he was in a car in the driveway. He had married a 19-year-old woman and was living with his brother in Florida. I didn't see him anymore until I was married and had children of my own.

After my grandfather wasn't living with us anymore, my mom gave the bed that was downstairs to my uncle, and she let me turn the basement into a skating area. I took my record player downstairs, and I would roller skate for hours. My stepdad was no longer allowed to come to the basement when I was skating down there. He never touched me again, and we didn't speak of what he had done. He would still try to watch me undress, and he was forever leaving the door ajar, hoping I would look at him. I tried to stay at a friend's house as much as possible, and always tried to stay at Granny's during the long holidays and summer. By the time I was nine years old and staying at Granny's, attending Vacation Bible School, and reading John 9, I had come to know that God was real.

CHAPTER FOUR

When my brother started high school, I would go to work with Mom and wait in the break room until she could drive me to school. She would take her break, drive me to school, and then go back to work. In the afternoons, we rode the bus home. Some days, my brother would drive me to school and when I would get out of his car, my chest and head would be vibrating from the music. I thought it was cool and so did my friends, but it didn't happen often because he wasn't home very much.

I had started playing softball and some days, I would stay over for practice. On the weekends, Mom would drop my brother and I off at the pool during the day and at the skating rink during the evening. When my brother started driving his own car, he didn't go with me to the pool or skating anymore, because he was much older and had his own friends. Mom always seemed to be happy when my brother was around, and I always felt that in her eyes, he could do nothing wrong.

We would go to see Daddy every now and then, until

my brother came home with bruises on his backside from where my dad had hit him. Then, my brother didn't go to visit with my dad at his house anymore. We would go to see Granny, and Daddy would sometimes show up. I was always glad to see him, but he never stayed very long, only a few minutes.

Grandpa would come over and pick us up from Granny's and we would spend the night with him and his wife. We always had a fun time there. His wife would let us eat cocoa with marshmallows out of the can and my brother got to play on the big dozers out back. He loved to drive them. Grandpa would take us back to Granny's where he would spend hours talking to her at the table. I treasured the times I stayed at my cousins, Granny's house, or a neighbor because then I got to go to church. It is strange that some of the hardest years of your life turn out to be the ones you learn the most from. When I look back on my childhood now, I choose to relive the good days, not the bad. You have a choice, too.

As I grew older, my brother was gone more and more, and Mom was letting me stay with family or friends on the weekends and summer so I wouldn't be at home alone with my stepdad very much. We moved again to a home away from my friends, but my mom kept us at the same school district. My brother was now driving all the time and hardly ever came home. I missed him so much. Also, I had gotten sick with my stomach, repeated 4th grade, had to go on Zantac, and change my diet.

It was spring when we moved. The house they had rented was older and cold at times. My brother's bedroom was little more than a closet. There was a small building beside the house attached to it and then the garage. The front yard had split-rail fencing and rose bushes on each area of the fence. The house also had a basement with a wood stove.

By this time, I was twelve. I had started my menstrual cycle and had taken an interest in the opposite sex. It wasn't very long before I found neighborhood friends. We had an older lady that lived beside us near our back yard. She was a kind, godly person, was not more than four foot tall, and loved to crochet. I would go to church with her often and hang out with friends in the neighborhood. Mom would tell me to be home before dark. I am not sure she ever really knew where I was.

I remember that Christmas, I wanted a juke box with lights on it. My brother helped my mom carry it upstairs, and it awakened me. I saw them carry it through the back door but when my mom came to check on me, I acted like I was asleep. I no longer believed in Santa. This was in the same house where my mom and brother were sitting at the kitchen table when he told her that his girlfriend was pregnant.

My stepdad came and picked me up after school the following week. I asked where Mom was, and he replied, "Sleeping." When I came home, she was sleeping in bed, and she had taken a whole bottle of Tylenol. I could not wake her, but I could tell that she was breathing. I begged my stepdad to call an ambulance, but he wouldn't. He said, "She will be fine, just let her sleep." I started screaming for my brother and I screamed until I could scream no longer. I do remember that my brother came home and stayed for the next two days. We didn't leave Mom's side. She woke up not knowing what had happened and we never talked about what took place.

My brother got married after this, and he moved to where his wife's family lived. A couple of weeks later, I developed shingles. They ran from my back to my chest and were very painful. I slept in my brother's old room and didn't miss any school. I did not want to be home anymore than I had to be.

CHAPTER FIVE

We had moved again back over near my old neighborhood. I was so happy to be back near my friends and riding the bus again. Many mornings I would wake up and my stepdad would be standing at my bedroom door watching me. No matter how many times I locked my door, he would find a way to open it or would be standing outside my bedroom window watching me.

I knew he had to be the one cutting my speaker and radio wires, but I had watched my brother and knew how to fix that. I learned how to bar my door, black out my windows, splice wires, create a hiding place in my closet, and how to get in and out of my room and the house without anyone knowing.

When I came home from school, Mom would be sleeping or in her closet crying with the door locked. I would get her to open the door and I would help her into bed. She would get back up during the evening and take a bath and sometimes, cook supper. During the evening, she would do her nails and lay out her clothes for the next day.

On Friday's, Mom picked me up from school. She would stop at the pharmacy to pick up medicine or whatever we needed, and we would go out for supper. On Saturdays, I went swimming and skating. On Sundays, she would always watch Billy Graham, lay in the sun, and clean the house. My stepdad always did the grocery shopping, but Mom would always get the cleaning supplies for our home. My mom always made sure we went shopping together and she always encouraged us to play sports and in the band. Sometimes, months would go past, and she would be okay. There was still yelling at times, and crying, but not as often.

By this time, I had a regular boyfriend that I had met at the skating rink. We had been boyfriend and girlfriend for almost two years, and I cared for him a lot. He had given me a promise ring for Christmas that year, but he didn't know my past. In school, I was a strong independent athlete that stood up to bullies but at home, I kept to myself, walking on eggshells until I could see how Momma was.

One evening, his brother drove us to a friend's house and we hung out as people do. Then, we went back to his brother's place. Things progressed and we had sex. I was thirteen years old, and didn't have a clue what I was doing. After it was over, I started to cry, and I couldn't stop crying. I was still crying when he took me home and when I saw my stepfather, I started screaming.

Mom took me in my bedroom and called my brother on the phone to come over as soon as possible. I could hear them talking to my date in the living room. He told them what had happened, and kept asking them if he could see me, and they kept telling him to leave. My brother came over and gave me one of Moms' pills, which caused me to fall asleep.

I talked with my boyfriend a few days later. I told him I didn't know what was wrong, I just didn't feel well. I stayed that weekend at a friend's house, and we went skating. I ran into my so-called boyfriend who was there with another girl. So, I threw his ring at him and never looked back.

When I went home the next day, Mom and I had gone to the store. When we were on the way back home, she asked me what was wrong, and I started to cry. I told her about what happened, and I told her again what my stepdad had done to me and how he was still tormenting me by trying to watch me and by cutting my speaker wires. As we pulled into the driveway, she slapped me and called me a liar. I got out of the car, ran into the house, and barred my door. I could hear my mom and stepdad yelling at each other and so, I just turned my radio volume up to drown them out.

When the house got quiet, I came out of my room.

Mom was in the living room, and I was headed toward the kitchen to get a drink. She stood up to come into the kitchen where I was. She saw my stepdad through the door, sitting in the driveway in his car with a hose run from the exhaust pipe through the window of the car, and she opened the door and went to stop him. I stayed inside. I didn't care if he died. I wanted him to die. I was upset that she stopped him and when I saw him start to get out of the car, I went back to my room.

The next few weeks, I went to school, came home, and went to my room until he went to bed. But God had a plan. Many years later, my stepfather sorrowfully repented of his sins. In his brokenness, he confessed to God and to my mom all that he had done to me and then, he asked for my forgiveness. I explained to him that through Christ I had forgiven him already and that Christ heals all wounds in His time.

When I started to walk with the LORD, God gave me the grace to forgive my stepfather of all that he had done to me. I needed to move on with my life, even without his confession or request for forgiveness. When someone accepts salvation, they are a changed person; a kind and caring person, who no longer thinks of themselves, but only wants to please God.

CHAPTER SIX

In May of the year that I was 14 years old, I met the father of my children, my first husband. I did not wait on God to plan for me. I was young, and I thought I knew it all.

My home was located beside the dragstrip. I had gotten a job running hotdogs and BBQ sandwiches from one tower to the other. The evenings were loud and full of white smoke from tire burnouts. My stepdad was working on the starting line, and we had begun talking again. He had halfway apologized to me, but my mom didn't apologize until much later in my life.

My husband-to-be was at the dragstrip with a friend. His friend was dating my friend at the time. We talked all the time he was in his first year at college and working at an ice cream store. I was going into 9th grade, playing softball, and thought I knew all there was to know. He would come to my house when he wasn't at college. During the weekend, Mom would let me ride the bus up the mountain to where he was in school and when my classes started, I would take the bus back to school.

He was kind and caring. He would send me flowers all the time. I was head over heels for him. I had told him all about my past. I didn't want to hide anything from him. That August, I turned 15 years old, and he came to my party. The following Friday, my mom and stepdad went to dinner and when they came home, they thought I was asleep inside my room, but I had crawled out of my bedroom window to meet my boyfriend in my front yard. We walked for a couple of hours until it was dark. We had sex for the first time on the grass outside my home. I remember how warm the night was and how sweet the grass smelled. I was so happy to be with him, and I felt like we could conquer the world. I would go to his house after this, and he would come to mine. We agreed that if I got pregnant, we would do what was right and get married. We went to church several times with his grandmother. He said that he thought he may want to be a preacher one day. His grandparents had raised him because his mom had abandoned him at the hospital. He never knew his father. We talked about children, and he was determined that his children would not work in a factory or do plant work.

We moved again about four miles from where we were living. It was in this home, in my bedroom, that I became pregnant with my first child. It was in

November, 1984.

A couple of months passed, and Mom asked me if I was okay. She said she could tell that something was wrong because I hadn't used any pads for my monthly. I told her I wasn't sure, but I was sick during the morning time, and hadn't felt well. She started screaming at me. "I trusted you!" she said. Then she said, "If you are pregnant, you are having an abortion, and you will never see him again!" Of course, I told her she wasn't going to make me do anything. When she took me to school that morning, she said, "I will be back to pick you up at lunch, and you be ready! I said, "For what?" She said, "We are going to the health department to get you tested." At lunch, she signed me out of school, and we went to the health department for bloodwork. I was two months pregnant.

She wouldn't speak to me on the way home. She made me get out of the car when we pulled up to the house and she went to my brother's. He said she was so angry that she ran her car into a ditch coming up his driveway. When she came home, I was trying to tell her that we were going to get married, but she refused to hear me or let me talk to him.

The next few days, my boyfriend would come to school to see me and one day, I left school and went to his house to tell his grandparents. His grandfather was so upset that he took his belt off and tried to beat my boyfriend in the yard. I just started crying and his grandmother took me in the house. In a short while they came into the house, and he drove me home.

When I came in the door, Mom said, "Get ready! You are going to your aunt's to have an abortion." I told her, "You can take me to my aunt's, and you can make me go to the doctor, but you cannot and will not make me ever give up my child." I was very stubborn and strong-willed. The next day, I came home from school and called my dad and told him I was pregnant. I asked him if he would sign for me to get married. He said that if that was what I wanted, he would sign. When my mom came home, I told her what I did, and she was livid. I couldn't wait to get away from her and that house. In a few days, she cooled off and agreed to let me talk to my boyfriend on the phone.

By this time, everyone knew that I was pregnant, and my grandmother was coming for Christmas. My brother and his wife were expecting their second child any day and so, things had started to calm down. We had arranged to get married in a church beside my uncle and aunt's house on January 26th, but we had to change it to the 27th because Granny wanted to get her hair done.

I was so happy and felt so loved. Mom, Granny, and I went shopping for my wedding dress right after

Christmas and my niece was born. Granny went home, and I prepared for my wedding. The girls all wore pink, and the boys all wore blue. My dad came to walk me down the aisle. Granny was crying, as was most of my family. She gave me $800 that she had saved for me. On my husband's side of the church was his aunt and his grandmother and his best friend's mom. His best friend was the best man, and my cousins made up the rest of the wedding party, except for my best friend, who was my maid of honor. That night we stayed in a hotel in Hickory, NC, and the next day we bought a car with the $800 that Granny had given me.

Then we moved into our first apartment. We had no idea about money or what things cost, or how to budget or manage money. We didn't know anything about taking care of a home, car, or what it was like to have to get up each day and go to work to support a family. I didn't know how to be a wife or a mother, and he didn't know how to be a husband, a dad, or a good provider. Only time, experience, and age teach you these things. All we knew was things were hard, lots of money was needed, and it was nothing that we expected it to be. The stress was unbelievable and at times unbearable.

He knew how to hit and fight his way through angry times, and I knew how to scream, cry, hold a grudge, and sometimes hit back. Mom and Granny came over to take me shopping. I didn't have a clue how or what to buy. It was the first time I had ever shopped for food, cleaning supplies, or toiletries. I didn't know how to cook anything except fried taters, cinnamon toast, and peanut butter cookies. My stepdad refused to let me do anything in the kitchen when he was around.

We were in the apartment for a few days fixing the bed I had brought from my room because I wanted my things. My husband, the loving and kind person I had dated, became angry and slapped me. I went to the other room, and he came in and started apologizing. He told me he was sorry, and that it wouldn't happen again. And it didn't… for a while. Once the abuse starts, the devil is let in and unless that person becomes saved, the abuse will not stop.

We were only there for three weeks because we couldn't afford the apartment. I tried to continue going to school, and we moved in with his aunt. In March, I was too big to fit in my desk. One day, not much later, the principal called me into his office and told me that I was a disgrace to the school because I was an athlete and was pregnant. He said that I needed to go home and stay there. He then sent me to the guidance counselor, who told me that I could continue my schoolwork at home and that they would send someone to the house to help me.

I went home and three weeks later, a lady arrived at

the door with some books. She came in and sat down. She started by explaining what I would need to do, and I asked if I was going to pass this year. She said that I was too far behind to catch up. I asked her to leave and not come back. She left the books. I returned them to the school later.

I was broken and devastated. I wanted to see Granny more than anything. I wanted to go to my safe place. I wanted to go home and lay down in her bed with my head on her side and sleep and never wake up. Mom showed up a couple of days later and she wanted me to come sit in her car, so I did. She told me what a disappointment I was to her and that she was disowning me as her daughter. I was so hurt that I told her I never wanted to see her again.

Out of abuse and yelling at each other only comes anger and hurt but when it is all you know, then that is what you use. This was the second time that I had stood up to my mom, and it was the first time and the last time I would say to her that I never wanted to see her again. God's plans are always greater than ours. No matter how much you think you have messed up your life He is ready to help you start anew. Trust Him.

We eventually moved into an apartment, not too far from Mom. My husband went to work at a furniture plant working in staining. Mom eventually came to visit a few times while he was at work, but she didn't stay long. I could see on her face how disappointed she was with me.

We had purchased an antique wringer washer. The kind with a barrel for the washer part and an electric wringer you place the clothes in to get the soap and water out. The washer worked well but the water was heavy and so were the clothes. I had a small circle clothesline outside.

In early June, we went to visit Granny. How happy I was to spend time with her. She was working in the garden as she had done when I was little. I convinced my husband to let me stay a week with Granny. I wasn't driving yet, so Granny and I walked to town to buy groceries and took a cab back to her house. This was one of the more precious times I remember. During the day, we worked in the garden and then, we would eat lunch. After lunch, she would take out her red hymnal and we would sing the songs I had heard all my life, the songs of Zion. During the evening, she would teach me to cook and after supper, we did the dishes together and she read to me from the scriptures. We talked about all she had seen in her lifetime. How her family came from the mountains on horse and buggy, down a steep rugged path to find work in an apple orchard. The week was gone in just minutes. I think I must have cried all the way back to the apartment. We only lived 45 minutes apart, but it felt like a million miles. I deeply craved for the peace that was in her home and her life, and even though my mind wasn't there yet, God could hear my heart. He knew what I longed for.

I spent my days cleaning, trying to cook, and preparing for our baby. I played instrumental music on the radio, I read books, talked to my baby, and tried to rest. I turned 16 years old and then, 22 days later they induced my labor to give birth. Mom came in and told me she loved me, then she went to the waiting area. She said she could hear me screaming where she was waiting and had to leave.

My husband never left my side and eight hours later, our son was born. They placed him on my stomach and his dad cut the cord. They took our son to clean him up and told me to push gently. Blood started gushing and I felt faint. The doctor grabbed my bed and pulled the bottom of it up, so I was standing on my head. I passed out. When I came to the next day, they told me what happened.

My husband had not left my side, they said. Our son was perfect. I remember being so afraid that something would be wrong with my baby because of the abuse I had endured this far. In my mind, now I had given birth to his beautiful healthy son and the abuse would stop because this is what he wanted, a son. I was so happy.

Mom and Granny came to the hospital each day. I

was there for five days. Granny came home with us from the hospital to stay with me for a couple of weeks until I could care for my baby on my own. She taught me many things, like how to care for my child, change him, feed him, and bathe him. But most of all, her prayers gave me strength. She taught me how to pray and reminded me that God was listening.

While Granny was there, my husband was good to me and kind again. Oh, how I hoped and prayed it would last! I made a promise to myself and to God that I would endure anything to keep my child safe and for us to continue to be a family. I knew what it was like to not have a father, and I didn't want this for my child. I could make it work; I could fix it. The worst part of abuse is what I call the "false hope times." Weeks where he wouldn't hit me or sexually assault me, and it would give me false hope that he had changed and that my prayers had been answered. I was believing that I could fix it, rather than leaving it in Gods' hands. It would be almost 12 more years before I would completely trust Christ and the plans He had for me.

My mother-in-law and her common-law husband showed up a week after Granny left. They were what we refer to as vagabonds, past carny people who move from place to place, usually in a motor home. There was nothing godly about them, but her common-law husband loved my children as his own grandchildren. He was always kind to me and my children. I was thankful that my children would have a grandpa now, but this was not one that I wanted to have around.

My mother-in-law saw our son as a chance to be the perfect grandparent and tried to make up for not raising her own son. This was only my third time meeting her and I had seen her as a threat to me and my child. I was afraid she was going to take him because it seemed that in her eyes, I could do nothing right. According to her, I was "Too young to have a child." My husband was even more upset by her visit. He said she was trying to make up for not being there to care for him as a baby. He said when he was a boy, she had only come for birthdays and graduations and that every year, they would leave for the winter and go to Florida. That was why she wasn't at our wedding. He said she had left him in the hospital and her mother, Mamaw, had to go get him and she was the only mother he had ever had. I asked about his father, and he said that he didn't know him and that he had tried to ask her about his father, but she refused to answer. He died inside not knowing his father.

We really didn't know each other's childhood or past very well. I had told him about the sexual abuse, but I had not shared with him about Mom. I wasn't sure what was wrong with her because some days she was normal and other days like a roller-coaster. Friendly one minute, what we call the high times and then cursing you out, crying and locking herself in the closet, what we called the down times.

CHAPTER SEVEN

In the weeks that followed my son's birth, we went to visit his grandparents. While driving to see them, a drunk driver came across the center line and hit us head on. We were not wearing seat belts, and our son was buckled in a carrier. My nose hit the rearview mirror and my head hit above the mirror on the top of the car. My arm hit the dash in front of me causing a huge bruise that looked like a break. Glass was everywhere. Our son was crying, and I could see a couple of small cut marks on his head. I got out and sat down beside the car, still in a daze. My husband got our son out of the car, still in his seat, and set him beside me. He went back to the car to open the trunk and fire engulfed the car.

When the ambulance came, the driver loaded me with my son on my stomach so that he would calm down. They kept asking my husband if he was okay, and he kept responding that he was fine. The driver of the ambulance said that we were lucky because the other driver was in a truck and drunk. He didn't have any injuries. Our son was checked and x-rayed head to toe. He only had a few scratches on his head and a knot on his collar bone where it had cracked and healed on its own. They said it happened during his birth. The doctor said that my arm was just badly bruised and I had broken the tip off my nose, but I would be fine. They told us that if our son had been in a regular car seat during the wreck, he would have been cut to pieces but because he was in the smaller, shorter seat, the glass pieces went over his head.

The car was towed to a car lot. We were allowed to go to the car to remove any belongings. As we approached the car, we could see the windshield on the driver's side had been completely broken with a large indentation. The man at the lot told us that my husband's head had hit the windshield so hard that it had completely busted the windshield. When I look back on my life, I see Christ protecting me and providing for me and my family all the way. I can hear people praying. I can see the prayers that were answered now.

After the car accident, we moved in with his grandparents. Our child was three months old. His grandmother, Mamaw, was a godly, praying woman full of faith. She had moved out of her room into my husband's old room to give us more space. She is also the one that introduced me to burnt popcorn. Man, is it good when you have an upset stomach.

As I mentioned before, since the time I was 10 years old, I had started having trouble with my stomach. When Mom took me to the doctor, they said I had stomach ulcers and prescribed Zantac and a strict diet of baked, boiled, or grilled food. They said it was because of the stress level at home. Since it was my mother's doctor, he already knew the situation.

Many nights at Mamaw's, my son and I would go and sit in her room and watch spiritual tv. During a spiritual tv program one night, I asked the LORD to heal my stomach, and He did! My ulcer was gone, and did not return.

Some nights, she would be on the phone for hours. I could hear her asking people if they were saved or if they would like to receive salvation by praying the sinner's prayer. I asked her how she knew who to call and she said, "I don't, I just call each number in the phone book until someone answers." She said that sometimes people answer and sometimes they don't, and if they are saved or receive salvation, I write it down with a date, so I don't call and ask them again. She went onto say, "Sometimes, people curse at me or hang up and that's okay. I pray that the LORD works on them." Then she told me to look behind the door. There, I could see a stack of phonebooks and notebooks about 4 feet tall. I remember thinking to myself, "Who will continue her work when she is no longer here? Who will reach these people?"

What a blessing she was to my life and although she died while my children were young, I know without a doubt she prayed daily for all of us. Not long before she passed, she told me that she had once had an out-of-body experience. I asked what she meant, and she said, "I was laying in the bed, and I could see my body, but I was also above my body floating in the room. I was reminded of my grandma saying to her children in the hospital, 'Do you see Him? There He comes.'" Then she was gone. I know without a doubt that I will see them both again in Heaven. God sends people into your life to help you grow in knowledge and faith of Him.

During my follow up appointment after giving birth to my son, I had decided to take birth control pills. I will not forget the name: Othonova. My husband loved Chevy Nova cars, and in his mind, the faster the better. We lived in one big bedroom, just off the kitchen of his Mamaw's house. He had taken a position working in shipping and receiving, and I stayed at home with our child until he was a year old. The abuse was still bad, but when Mamaw heard me scream, she would try to come in the door to help me. More than one time, I thought he would kill me. His childhood best friend lived across the street and many times, he would stay out late with him drinking and then come home and pass out.

When he was out or passed out, it was peaceful. I became pregnant with our daughter while taking the pill, when our son was only nine months old.

I was 17 years old, had a child, and was three months pregnant when I went to work in a sewing shop. I worked sewing baby clothes together. They called it working on production. Starting pay was $3.10 per hour, but I could make production because Granny had taught me how to sew on her machine. So, I was making good money.

I prayed every night that my little girl would be nothing like me. I prayed that she would be strong and independent so that no man would ever run over her. I prayed that she would be just like my cousin, and I prayed that her birth would be easier.

I refused to go to the doctor until I was seven months along. To me, if something was wrong with my child, then I didn't want to know because I wasn't giving her up and no one was taking her away from me. I cried a lot and prayed a lot.

I was in labor only three hours when our healthy baby girl was born. She was born in the middle of the night and they let me come home the next day after supper. A few days later, Mom came to visit and she was so upset at where we were living that she only stayed a few minutes. I went back to work when our daughter was six weeks old. Thank goodness Mamaw was there to babysit. Our baby girl had her days and nights mixed up. We tried everything to keep her awake during the day. We even tried flipping her upside down. It didn't work. When she was six months old, she changed it herself.

I was let go at the sewing plant because they lacked work. The whole company was laid off and eventually closed. Our jobs had started going overseas. Mom had started on a new medication and helped me to get a position at the same nursing home where she was working. I rode back and forth to work with Momma and in time, we started to grow closer and closer.

When I was 18 years old, I finally got my driver's license and started driving. My mom had my stepdad sign for me to get a car. I made payments to the company, not him. We always went to Mom's for Christmas Day. My brother would come with his wife and three children and us with our two children.

My brother and his wife were only together for six years before he had to move out. She had several boyfriends. He took the children and moved in with my mom. My mom was working second shift now, and my brother was working first shift, and his youngest was still in a walker. I went to visit and was sitting at the table, holding my daughter, watching the other children play. My mom told my brother that it was too much for her, and that he was going to have to give the children back to their mother. He was so broken. He took the children and left. I went home. I didn't understand at that time that my mom was learning how to talk to express when something was too much for her or when she was feeling overwhelmed. Years later, I understood what it meant to have a breakdown and become depressed, but by the time I came to understand this, it had a name and lots of different choices of medication to treat the problem.

A couple of weeks later, I took the children to see Granny at her house for the weekend. My brother was there repairing her cabinets and had his oldest son with him. We were always at home at her house. We laughed and cut up. We had the best time repairing and cleaning. My brother left on Saturday evening to go home while we stayed and went to church with Granny.

That Sunday after church, we were sitting on the front porch swing. I wanted so much to tell her about the abuse, but I couldn't tell her all of it. I told her we were arguing and having trouble getting along with each other. She said, "You made your bed, you must lay in it." I understood that I was to stay married. It took me a long time to get past her words. I should have told her the whole truth, but I never did. I was taught by her and others in my family that divorce was a last option, and if you did divorce then you didn't remarry until your spouse was dead.

It would be many years later before I would understand that God does not desire for His children to tolerate abuse from a spouse and that it is not normal or okay. I was listening to the radio when I heard the speaker say, "God is your Father." He loved you so much that He sent His only Son to die for your sins. Now think of how much you love your children and how you never want to see them hurt and think to yourself, you are human, how much more do you think God loves you, why would you ever think that He would want you to stay in a situation where you or your children are being abused?" God was speaking to me, and I felt it.

We had moved into a mobile home close to Mom and my stepfather. My husband's car wasn't working and was parked at his friend's house. I was still working at the nursing home with Mom. My husband had started working second shift at a printing company, I was still working first shift and things were quieter around the house, but the weekends were still hard. I called this mobile home the House of Mice. We had lots of mice in this home and at nighttime, they would go across your body while you were sleeping. We tried everything to get rid of them.

One night my husband came home, and I was asleep because I was so tired. He wanted me to get up and cook supper for him. We got into a huge argument, with lots of screaming and fighting. The neighbors called the police. My husband took my car and left me at home with the children. I was so scared that I walked with the children in the dark night to the landlord's house and had them call Papaw to come get us.

The children and I went back to his grandparents' house. Three days later, my husband showed up. The abuse stopped for a few months. Even though we were living near Mom, I would not go to her place for safety. Sometimes, I would go to visit my mom, but I made it plain to her that she would never be allowed to watch my children alone in her home and that I would never leave them unattended with her if her husband was around. She never asked me to let the children stay at her house as long as he lived. When the children were older, she would come and stay with them at my house.

My mom was a wonderful grandma, but for the life of me to this day, I can't understand how she could have stayed with her husband knowing what he had done to me. We missed out on so much precious time together. So many mother-daughter things that we didn't do were robbed from us. Later, she would come and tell me what a great parent I was and how she wished she would have been stronger. God's greatest gift to us besides His salvation, is forgiveness and love with those who have hurt us.

CHAPTER EIGHT

When our daughter was two and our son had just turned four, I went to the doctor to ask about having my tubes tied. He said that my husband or mother would have to sign because I was under 21 years old. My husband flat-out refused, so Mom went with me. I went to the hospital that morning and came home that afternoon. Back then, they made a 4-inch incision across your hair line to do the procedure. It took me a few weeks before I could stand up straight and walk. I had my tubes burnt and tied. I wanted to make sure that I would have no more children with him, ever. If it hadn't been for Mamaw, I would not have made it. Time and time again, she helped me walk through the house and care for my children.

While living with his grandparents this time, we saved and bought a used two-bedroom, one-bathroom mobile home. It came with a washer and dryer and a hole in the kitchen floor that had to be repaired. We had rented some land about five miles from my husband's work, and that is where our first mobile home was situated. It had a small front porch and a deck with a chimney from an old torn down house in the back for a porch. We hooked up the septic and had a pole for the power, but it was never hooked up.

There was a creek in our front yard with a long field on the other side that stretched all the way to the highway. On the left of us was a spring. We had an oil heater that Granny had given us and a gas stove in the kitchen that my mother-in-law had given us. The oil circulator we used for heat was located in the living room. The oil barrel that fed the circulator was outside on a deck that used to be a part of an old house. We used gas lanterns in the rooms to see at night.

By this time, the children were three and four years old, and they shared a room with bunk beds at one end of the mobile home, while our room was at the other end.

It was springtime when we moved there. At nighttime, you could look out at the trees that lined the front yard and see thousands of lightning bugs. We carried water from the spring into the house to use and when it was warm out, I played with the children in the creek in the front yard.

Six months later, I quit working at the nursing home and stayed home with my children. We had no TV, only books. So at night, when my husband was at work, I would read and play with my children. It was so peaceful. We didn't have the noise of the outside world.

Yes, these were hard times and there would be more to come, but through these times, God was molding me into being Christ-like. You see, no matter what we go through in our lives, we all crave the same things: love, peace, joy, and stability. We search and search for this continually until we meet the LORD and then, we realize it is all in Him. It is not within this world or any person in this world. The only way you will ever be satisfied in this world is in and through knowing Christ. Your happiness will never last in this world because you are only passing through here. Our real home in Heaven is eternal. Our home is in Heaven with our God who is peace, love, and joy unending. All the things we crave here, we have waiting for us there.

Christmas came and went. We stayed in our mobile home as much as possible, but when it became too cold, we would stay at his grandparents. We were gone for three weeks during January that year and so, someone broke into our home, taking most of my things and of course, threw all of our belongings on the floor.

A few months passed and then, my husband was going to be laid off. The printing businesses were going to close and move overseas. He came home wanting our birth certificates and I said that I wouldn't give them to him until he told me why. He said that he had been talking to a recruiter and that he had to go take a test, but they needed our birth certificates. He said that he would be doing the same job he had been doing at the printing shop. I gave him the papers and he left. When he returned several hours later, he said we are going in the military. I said you may be, but we are not going.

For the next few weeks, he was kind like he had been when we were dating. We put our mobile home up for sale. It sold in four days, and we moved back to his grandparents' house, but this time was different. His aunt and her children had moved into the room where we had stayed. His grandfather had just finished building what he called a "meat room." It was a 20-foot by 40-foot deck with a 12-foot by 20-foot room built on part of it. The room had no electricity and no plumbing. It wasn't attached to the house, but it was within 6 feet of it. This was to be where my children and I would live until we moved near a military base.

We stored all our belongings on the covered deck except what we needed for everyday use. Things we use every day were brought in the room along with the children's bunk beds to sleep on. Papaw had a refrigerator on the deck just outside the door of what we called the "apartment." He had built a counter and placed a brown sink in it with a bucket underneath to catch the water, and I brought my brown gas stove from the mobile home.

Our son was starting school. We had no heat, no air conditioning, and we went into the house to use the bathroom. I didn't care because in two weeks, my husband would be gone, the abuse would stop, and my children and I would be safe.

CHAPTER NINE

This is just a small portion of my childhood and young life. It is my belief that you only grow in hard times because in the good times, you are not talking as much with the LORD or spending as much time with Him. In the hard times, He is molding you to be more like Him.

I will tell you that years later, my children's father came to know the LORD. He developed pancreatic cancer when he was 40 years old and accepted the LORD into his heart just days before he died.

You must hide what the LORD tells you in your heart and keep it there. When you need His words, in your darkest hours, He will bring it to your mind. Even in our lowest times, God is watching and working for us. Often, we can't see it until later, but He is always there. He will never leave you or forsake you. He will go with you all the way if you let Him.

The children and I remained in the small meat room for six months. Their father went through boot camp and then AIT school, and I swore to myself that I would not join him when he finished his training. He sent letters home every week apologizing, saying how sorry he was for the way he had treated me, and how he would never do that again. I tried to be gone when I knew it was time for him to call. I was determined to stay where I was and find a place that I could afford on my own with my children.

I had started working again at another sewing plant. We made baby clothes, and I was making a pretty decent paycheck. On the weekends and holidays, we went to visit Granny and sometimes Momma. I would take our clothes to their house to wash them.

We spent the whole week with Granny during the Fourth of July. Her health had started to fail, and she had been staying with her sister, even though both of them were starting to decline. She was always so excited to go home even if it was only for a few days. I was so happy to be with her and my children. We went to church with her each Sunday when we were there. We would take drives just to see the mountains and enjoy the ride. Oh my, how I miss her and her wisdom.

She took this time to talk with me more about growing old, having faith in God, and trusting Him in all things. When I was with her and listening to her speak of Christ and His love for her, my heart was filled with joy. She spoke of her mother and father and how there were ten of them traveling in a covered wagon off the mountain, down to the foothills to find work in apple orchards and a sawmill to survive. She said she had a baby brother and a baby sister that didn't make it. They were buried across the mountain. I took her to visit their graves. She said times had been hard, but God was good, and He had provided food, jobs, and clothing for them.

There were very few things they got to carry with them, but the sewing machine I have today was one of them. Granny taught me to sew on the machine just as her mom had taught her. Many quilts and much clothing were made from that old paddle machine. She said that they were so proud to be working. As I think of the sewing today and how her hands held the material with such careful thought to where the next stitch should go for the material to be used for a quilt or a garment, I see how our Heavenly Father is shaping us into what we are to be. Trimming pieces here and there so that we fit perfectly into the plan that He has for our lives. We all have curves in our lives, extra pieces we can't place, or times that we stop moving forward when we shouldn't. But when the Master sewer takes hold of us, He corrects our steps and places us back on the correct path that leads to the way home.

I recall the winter in the meat room and looking back on it now, all I can say is that God in His loving kindness and mercy, has seen us through it all. I can't tell you why the place we were living didn't burn down or why we didn't freeze to death with no insulation and only a small kerosene stove to keep us warm. The snow was so deep that year and winter seemed to last forever. It was so cold most nights that I sent the children into the house to sleep in a room with Mamaw. I was so afraid that they would freeze to death. I stayed in the meat room by myself, in the children's bunkbeds with piles of covers on top of me. I prayed that my husband would not return if I wasn't supposed to be with him, and I prayed that if he did return, he would be the kind and caring person that I had once dated.

We went to visit him one time after bootcamp and before AIT school for three days. He seemed to be changed, but I was distant and guarded. In my mind, I knew that anyone could change for three days. I wouldn't talk to him on the phone after we returned home. I had written him a letter telling him that I was not going with him to Fort Bragg.

In the spring when he finally returned home, he said he was a changed man and that he would never hurt me again. I believed him. After all, I had asked the LORD to not let him return if we were not supposed to be together. The children were happy to see their dad and I was full of hope. We drove down to Fort Bragg and found a place to rent. It was our first home away from our parents and grandparents with our own little family. Plus, it had running water and electricity. We were so happy. I had started reading my little white Bible that Granny had given me, and the LORD started opening my eyes to things I had not seen before. I would pray with my children each night before bed; just simple prayers, like "now I lay me down to sleep," and "God watch over the individuals name, In Jesus name, Amen."

We lived there for a year. Our daughter was starting school, and I was feeling bad that I hadn't finished high school. I inquired about finishing my GED and wouldn't you know it, the classes being offered were within walking distance of our home. Every day, I put my children on the bus and then, I walked to school. I finished my GED in one year during the evenings, and I worked at a restaurant near our home most weekends. The children came to work with me during the weekend. The family who owned the restaurant became my family. God's hand is always working.

We decided to try to buy a mobile home closer to base and then at the restaurant, I somehow ran into this lady that told me that she and her husband had received orders to go to Germany. They were making payments on a mobile home close to the base and it was almost paid for. All they wanted was someone to take over the payments. Can you say prayer answered!?! I took over the payments for the mobile home and left my husband to get away from the abuse. Within two months, I had finished school, bought a second car, and we were buying a home. Life was good and so was their father. I was drawing closer and closer to the LORD and had started reading more of my Bible to the children. I could feel myself starting a new journey and I had started to settle into life.

The restaurant closed, but the lady who ran it and I had taken a job together at a sewing factory. She was Catholic and I was so close to her that I called her Ma. She was like the mother that I never had but always wished for. I became close to her daughter, son, and their families. It was good to have close friends that I consider family.

We moved into our home and Mom and Granny came to watch me graduate. I had invited Daddy, but he said that he was too busy to come. I was heartbroken. I was the first to graduate high school in my family. I was so happy that I could now help my children with their classwork.

Mom and Granny stayed with us for four days and during this time, I saw the aggressive side of my husband that I hadn't seen in almost two and a half years. While they were visiting, I acted as though there was nothing wrong. I was ashamed of the choice I had made to trust him. After they left, things started again, slowly at first. He stopped both children from going out with me alone in the car because I know he was afraid that I would leave. He had every right to be worried because it was on my mind day and night.

He came home from work one evening and told me that we had to move to Germany. I told him that *he* had to move to Germany, but we were not going anywhere. That was a huge argument that lasted about three days. His Mamaw was sick with cancer during this time, and I guess that is why he didn't fight me harder about staying in the Army. He did not re-enlist. Instead, he took a position working at another printing company. The following year, Mamaw died. They threw away all her phone books and notes. I could imagine that all the people she had called and led to the LORD were greeting her in Heaven. I could hear them saying, "Remember when you called me and asked me if I wanted to receive the LORD, and how much He loves me?" Precious memories. What a blessing they are.

The following summer, the children started T-ball and my husband decided to coach. When he started coaching, I noticed how hard he was on our children and even more so on our son. I found a church to go to near our home. During Wednesday evening, they offered Bible classes for the children. I tried to go to church as a family on Sundays but most of the time, he would start a fight with me just so I would get upset and not go. He finally agreed to go three times but then, he told me that the children could go on Wednesday evening, but I was not permitted to go anymore. I tried several times to go but when I did, things turned very violent.

He had now started punishing the children with army punishments, making them hold a broom with arms stretched out and locked until the children felt like their arms would fall off. He did things to them to upset them just so I would get angry. He wanted to pick fights with me so that he would feel justified in hurting me. I let him have his way with me to keep him from hurting my children, but I did tell him one day, "You will look up and we will be gone." I told him that he should be thankful for his wife and children that love him. I kept praying and begging God to not let him come home.

He purchased a computer shortly after this and started playing computer games. I didn't care what he did. For a while, there was peace again, but I didn't insist on going to church anymore. Since I couldn't go to church, I would watch John Hagee on TV when I got home from work in the afternoons before my husband came home. One day, I don't even remember the sermon that was on TV. I just remember I fell on my face on the floor and all I could do was cry. In my mind I was praying, praying like never before. My heart felt like it was going to explode. I was begging the LORD to help me overcome the hurt and the pain and to show me what to do. God always answers prayers in His time.

I was always sure to call Granny once a week and after T-ball season was over, we went to visit Granny again. This time, I went with Mom and took my daughter with me. When we went in to pick her up, Granny had suffered a stroke that had left her mind unable to clean herself. We left her at the house with her sister, went to where my father was working, and explained to him the state that Granny was in. Together, we decided that she needed more care, and that she would need to go to the nursing home for a short stay so that they could work with her.

Granny, Momma, and I had all worked in nursing facilities and when we talked with her, she wanted to go. But when she got there, it was a lot different than working in one. I kept remembering what she had said to me and her words rang through me. She had said if I ever stop working, I will sit down and die. All that day, those words played over and over in my mind. The first two months of her stay at the nursing home, I would still go down and take her home when I could and when I couldn't take her, Momma did.

It had been another long winter and Daddy decided that we should think about doing something with Granny's house. I am sure the nursing home was pushing him to sell. We all met at Granny's house, and she said that she had things that she wanted to give us. I was given her mother's sewing machine, cast iron pans, and a quilt Granny had made for me. She asked me if there was anything else I wanted. I was so upset that I couldn't answer. I went outside to the porch swing. I just sat there crying and remembering all the lazy, warm days we sat on the swing talking and laughing. I thought of all the walks we took to town and back, and how during harvest we sat on the porch with her sisters and friends and strung beans. I thought back to all the hot nights and how she would fan me until I went to sleep.

Granny came out to the porch swing and sat down beside me to hold me. She said, "Don't cry, I have had a good life, and I know what is waiting ahead." Then she asked me if I wanted her house, our home. I told her that I couldn't be there without her, that it hurt too much. She told me that she understood, and that she loved me, and that it was going to be ok. After that, I left. The pain was too great. I cried all the way back to Fort Bragg but for once, I couldn't wait to get home. I know now, in hindsight, that I was running, trying to get away from the pain.

I was at our home in Fort Bragg and was preparing to go back and see Granny for the weekend. It was a Friday, and I had spoken to Granny on Thursday night to tell her that I was coming down on Friday evening after work. Mom called as I was getting ready to go to work and said, "I am over here with Granny, and she said you are coming down tonight, but you might want to come now. She doesn't feel well." Mom let me talk to her. I told her that I loved her and that I had to go to school to pick up the children and after that, I would be on the way. She said, "I love you, too, I will be waiting."

I immediately called the school and asked them to have the children ready for me to pick up because I had a family emergency. I left the house and went to their school, which was just minutes down the road, and picked them up. I came back to the house and was loading our clothes in the car when Momma called. I knew when I heard her voice that Granny was gone from this world. Mom said, "Granny kept asking when you would be here, and as we were talking, she just fell back on the bed." Mom continued with, "She was still breathing, and I told her you were on the way. The nursing home called the ambulance, and I rode with her to the hospital. Your dad met us there and the doctor came out of the ER, and told us that she had just died of congestive heart failure."

All I could do was cry. When my husband came home, I was still packed and all I wanted was to go be with Granny. He wouldn't let me go until the plans for her funeral were made. I stayed 15 minutes at the funeral home and then I had to leave. We went to the church where I had accepted the LORD many years before, and then to the graveyard. Granny had everything paid for and prearranged. It felt like an eternity.

We came back to Fort Bragg immediately after the graveyard service. I was glad to be home because at home it didn't feel like she was gone, and I felt like she was only a phone call away. Actually, a few days passed when I picked up the phone and dialed her number, and it took me a few seconds to realize that she wasn't going to answer.

That's when the brokenness started. I made it through the next few weeks feeling numb and going through the motions of day-to-day life. I awoke one day a few weeks later and could not stop crying. In my mind, my whole life was replaying like watching a movie backwards. My husband took me to the hospital, where they said that I was having a breakdown and to give me Benadryl every time I woke up. On Monday, I went to the psychiatrist and I told him that it was because Granny had died recently, and all about the abuse of my stepfather, and how my mom had a break down too. I did not mention my husband. I was afraid they would take my children and place them in foster care. He said I would be fine in a few weeks and sent me home with medication.

Over the next few weeks, I grew stronger and stronger in the LORD. I knew He would not leave me and that I would not have Granny back here sick in the nursing home. I began to feel powerful and strong in mind and body. 2 Corinthians 12:9 says, "And He said unto me, My grace is sufficient for thee: for my strength is made perfect in weakness. Most gladly therefore will I rather glory in my infirmities, that the power of Christ may rest upon me."

By this time, my children were 10 and 12 years old. One evening, my husband came home from work and wanted to go to Pizza-Hut. We arrived at the restaurant, and he started belittling me and talking mean to the children. In times past, I had tried to quiet him down, but this time was different. The waitress brought the drinks to the table and as she sat them down, I looked at my children and said, "Get in the car, we are leaving." He tried to grab my arm to make me sit down but I pulled away. We got in the car arguing and yelling all the way home with him speeding at 90 mph.

When we went into the house and he drew back to hit me in the kitchen, our son jumped between us. He picked him up and threw him against the refrigerator. The anger that welled up inside me was overwhelming and I instantly remembered where the handgun was. I had moved it behind the freezer. The LORD told me that my husband was not worth losing my children, so I moved our son out of harm's way. The children and I went to the living room, and he went to the bedroom. He knew he had crossed the line. That evening the children went to bed and I went to pray with them. They asked me if we could leave, and I told them to be ready the next morning because when they saw him go to work, I would come down and pick them up at the bus stop.

The next morning, he didn't go to work, he stayed home. I had not returned to work yet and so, all day he tried to apologize and tell me how sorry he was, and that it wouldn't happen again. I made him think everything was okay. I knew in my heart it was not going to be better.

The next day he went to work. I went and picked the children up from the bus stop. It took us 2 hours to pack all we could, including the cat and my sewing machine. Finally, we got on the road. I was constantly looking in the rear-view mirror, terrified that he would be behind us. I had managed to save $150 that he didn't know about. I left the checkbook, our home, and everything that wouldn't fit in the car. We went to the restaurant where Mom was working, and he was already calling everyone to find us. When Mom told me this, we went to my aunt's house. From there, I called a shelter, and we stayed there for six weeks until they could help us find a place to live.

The first night, the children both said listen to how quiet it is, no more yelling. We were able to hide from him for six months. When he found us, I moved again. We settled into an apartment, and I went back to work at a restaurant. Four months later he showed up. I looked at him in the face and said, "I will see you buried under the jail house before I move again." Then, I called the police.

That night my son slept on the floor between me and his sister. We had started reciting the LORD's prayer and that night, I prayed, "LORD, please make it real to me, help me to understand." I prayed with the children and then I began to pray for myself. I remember telling God, "I know I must trust You to take care of them. You gave them to me, and if You decide to take them back then, Your will be done, LORD, I will try to understand." A release came over my body and from that day on, I was not afraid of what my husband would do to us.

A year later, in my weakness, I started to go back to him. That lasted two days and then, I was totally finished. He moved to another state after that, and I continued raising my children. I will never be able to thank the LORD enough for all He has brought me through, and for all the courage and strength that He still gives me today.

CHAPTER TEN

Our son eventually joined the military and was stationed at Fort Bragg. I knew in my heart that he was safe there because I had not lost touch with the friends that had become our family. Today, he is retired from the military, has a family of his own, and works for the police force.

Our daughter grew up and graduated top of her class in law enforcement. She became a strong, independent woman who is not afraid to be herself. She now is married and has a family of her own. She encouraged me to write about my journey with the LORD.

As for me, I eventually got married again. I would like to tell you it lasted my lifetime, but it did not. So, after almost 20 years we parted as friends. Soon after this, I met my current husband. He had lost his wife. He brought me to Hinton, West Virginia, for vacation and I fell in love with life in this historic small town. We are happily married. We bought a house and we found a local church to attend. God is so good. He has given me more than I deserve or ever dared to dream.

There is a place in the Bible where it says, "I called on the LORD and He heard my prayers." I was terrified to marry again and when I met my current husband, I prayed, "LORD, if you don't want us together, take him away." It has taken me a long time to trust the LORD with my whole heart, but I know now whatever happens to me, I will serve Him, I will trust only Him, I will obey Him, and I will place my faith in Him alone. He will see me through, no matter the cost. In the good and in the bad, I will forever praise Him, for He is worthy of all.

Everyone's life is a journey of twists and turns and ups and downs. How you deal with these is your choice but remember, your choices bring you closer to Christ or take you further away from Him and the wonderful plan He has for you.

The stories I have shared are only a glimpse of the things that God has brought me through. I look back on my life now and see the mercy and grace that God has given to me. I see all the many, many times that He has watched over me and blessed me.

Whatever you are going through, He will make a way for you. He will always provide what you need. In Philippians 4, it does not say, "He will supply your wants or desires," it says, "needs." Often times in our lives, we do not understand this. I am sure that there will be times to come in my own life that I do not understand this. There might even be times when the pain is so great, or my heart is so broken that I will be yelling at God that I don't understand why. My only prayer is that I remember that I must trust Him. Truly, He is our only hope.

I have no doubt in my mind that He is real, and that He is always present. My feet are planted on the road to Heaven, and I know that whatever I face in this life, it will all be worth it when I get to my Heavenly home. The LORD has blessed me in so many ways. I see and feel His presence daily in my life. I will never be able to praise Him or thank Him enough!

Thank You, LORD, for giving me the courage to write this book. I pray it reaches many who are lost and hurt. I pray it blesses them and opens their eyes. I pray it fills their hearts with a love for You, LORD. I thank You, LORD, for my trials, because they have brought me closer to You. Thank You, LORD, for my family and friends who have supported me through my journey thus far, and I thank You most of all for my salvation. I know one day my eyes will see You.

CHAPTER ELEVEN

What prompted you to open this book? Can you confess to yourself about what is happening in your life right now? Are you still in a broken stage or have you moved onto the bitter stage? Are you stuck because the bitterness is like a snake that has bit you and won't let go?

Give it to God. There is brokenness in everyone's life. No matter how perfect the other person looks, they still have times of brokenness, times of sorrow, times of grief, times of love, times of joy, times of peace, times of conflict, and times of judgement. We are all human, and this is how it is to be alive on this earth.

You may feel like part of you is dead but it is just asleep. You must sleep to heal. We always start looking around at how other people's lives are when we become upset or feel we are missing something from our own life. What we are truly missing is why we exist.

God gave you the gift of life. In Jeremiah 15, the scripture talks about how the LORD knew you before He formed you in the womb. Think about that. We serve a God that is so powerful that He knows everyone and everything. He is all-knowing and chooses to love us anyway. He knew everything you would do, every bad thing, every good thing, every thought you would have, and He still allowed you to exist in this world. He is giving you a gift or an ability to help others find Christ. That is your sole purpose in this life: to lead others to Christ. My prayer is that reading this book will help to change your life and that you will feel led to follow Christ throughout all of your days.

I don't want to stand before the LORD and hear Him say, "Well, I had all of this planned for you but because you chose bitterness, I had to choose someone else to do what I had planned for you." You can't stop what the LORD has planned; He will just use a different person to get the job done. He loves you enough to let you choose to follow Him.

As I pointed out earlier, Jesus says in Revelation 3:20, "Behold, I stand at the door, and knock: if any man hear my voice, and open the door, I will come into him, and sup with him, and he with me." Jesus will not force His way into your life; it is your choice. You must open the door to invite Him.

The battle within you is between the devil and Christ. They are battling for your soul. The choice you make leads down the path you choose. You have to choose not to be bitter, not to hold a grudge, but you must choose to let the LORD fight the pain you feel. Trust the LORD to do what is best for you. You must lay down your burdens before the LORD.

When you are saved, the LORD Christ Jesus lives within you and He fights for you. Exodus 14:14 says, "The LORD shall fight for you, and ye shall hold your peace." We grew up with sayings such as, "what comes around goes around," or "they will get what is coming to them," and "karma comes back to bite you in the bottom." We should have been taught to let it go and keep walking with Christ. No battle is too big or too small for Him, but you must trust Him to handle it.

Life is so short, and I don't want to spend my energy and my time on people that are bitter and holding grudges, we are commanded to love one another as Christ loves us. Letting go of bitterness is not to help the other person. This is to help you. The LORD commands it because it is the way for us to be like Him. Look at all He has given for you.

I heard a preacher say one time that we hung the LORD on the cross and I thought to myself, "Well I wasn't there, so I didn't do that. I didn't pluck out his beard, beat Him until His skin was flayed, push a crown of thorns in His skull, pierce His hands and His feet with nails, and hang Him on a cross." But it was me and it was you, because He took all of the sins of the whole world on Himself so that we could have a free choice to love and trust Him. Your sins, my sins, the sins He knew that we were going to do even before we were born.

Think about how much He loves you, to suffer and die like this for you and for a world that hates Him. How loving and merciful He is that He has allowed us to live the way we do, running from Him time and again. And all the while, He is saying, "Come to me, lay those burdens down. I am your creator, I love you, I want you to choose to be with me in Heaven. Follow Me."

When you choose to be better, it doesn't happen right away. You still have to process things you were hurt by in this world. The healing process depends upon how badly and how deeply you were hurt. When it is just an acquaintance that hurt you, then you can let that go quickly; but when a person who promised to love, honor, and cherish you hurts you, or when the LORD decides to take a person out of this life and we feel it was too soon for their life to be over, the bitterness, anger, and hurt can become overwhelming.

The first question I always have is, "Why not me, LORD? I'm ready." We may look around and see a mean person or an older person and we question, "Why didn't you take them, LORD, instead of this person I loved?"

The next picture that pops into my brain is of all the people in the whole universe standing on two conveyor belts. One conveyor belt is going to Heaven and the other one is going to hell. We are all in place, people of all ages, sizes, and colors. We are placed on this belt when we become old enough to accept Christ as our savior or reject Him. The LORD has already seen into our future, and He knows all the choices we will make before we make them. He knows our heart. Hebrews 4:13 says, "Neither is there any creature that is not manifest in his sight: but all things are naked and open unto the eyes of him with whom we have to do." When it is time to go, then we must go to our eternal home. Death has no age, and it comes for all.

It is so important that you are ready to meet Jesus. I have walked with Him long enough to honestly say, no matter what I am going through, "LORD Jesus, I don't understand it, but I know it will be what is best for me and what will glorify You, LORD. I trust you."

You will still go through the process of grieving, sadness, shock, denial, anger, bargaining with God, depression, testing, and then acceptance of what has happened, but through all of this you must believe God and trust that He has a better plan for you and your life.

When you choose to stay bitter, you never move to acceptance, you are stuck in your bitterness, feeling sorry for yourself. When you choose acceptance then you will move on to forgiveness.

You start by asking the LORD for forgiveness. You will ask Him for forgiveness for not understanding His plan, and forgiveness for not trusting Him and that He has a better plan for you. You will ask Him for forgiveness of the anger you feel, and it may even be the anger you feel toward the LORD Himself.

This is also when you need to ask the LORD to help you to forgive the person who has wronged you. You may even ask the LORD to forgive you for the thoughts you have had while going through this loss and that is exactly what it is: a loss. It may not be a death of a person, but it is still a loss. This is why you still must go through the process to heal.

Now that you are here, where do you go next? You ask the LORD to help fill this hole in your heart with His love and get busy helping someone else. This stage of healing takes a while. You love someone because God commands it, but you hate what they have done to you, so you avoid them. You have told yourself, "I'm not going to talk to them, I'm going to avoid them because they will only hurt me again," and you put up a fence. This works for a little while, but then you realize you haven't placed the fence to keep them out; you placed the fence and it is confining you. It is keeping you in lockdown from living, from breathing, from laughing because it is taking all the joy from your life.

Then, you hear the LORD say, "Whatever weapon is formed against you, shall not prosper." (See Isaiah 54:17.) You soon realize that all you have been through has brought you closer to your Heavenly Father, and knowing this causes you to love the person who hurt you. This is a love God has grown in your heart. You begin to understand that you are closer and closer to home. You now know what unconditional love is. You realize and understand the kind of love that the LORD has for you.

This love goes beyond the boundaries of this world. This is a love that only Christ can place in your heart when you fully place your total trust in Him and in Him alone. You can then see Christ was with you all the way. He didn't leave you when you asked Him why. He never turned away from you. He held you and comforted you until it didn't matter why anymore. When you were at your most broken, He carried you. When you wanted to die and ask Him to please take you home to Heaven so the pain would stop, He whispered, "Just hold on, I have better plans in store for you. I am working on your behalf, my child, I do hear you." All the while He is saying, "Just place your trust in me. I will overcome. I will bring you through this. I have not left you. I have not fed you to the wolves."

Each new day brings a little bit more understanding

and newness to your life. You begin to understand what it truly means to walk with Christ. Your mind becomes constantly stayed on Him. You want to walk and talk with Him all day and night. Everything you do and with your whole being you want to glorify Him. He becomes your all in all. The fence you built around your heart is removed and then, whenever you start to fall again you hear Him say, "I will protect, you are mine, and man cannot harm you."

You now realize He has fought your battle for you, and you are the one who grew stronger because of it. There is nothing more this world can offer you. The world has no hold on you. Your life is now in Christ, and you only want what He wants for you. You know He will do what is best for you and what will glorify Him. Your best life is now in front of you. He heals all things in His time. If we healed ourselves in our time, we would never learn to trust Him. Romans 15:13 says, "Now the God of hope fill you with all joy and peace and believing, that ye may abound in hope, through the power of the Holy Ghost." If you haven't experienced the Holy Ghost in your life, ask the LORD to fill you full, and trust He will do as you ask of Him.

When you remember your past, you must see your way through to where you are now. There is a reason your eyes are in front of your head so that you keep walking forward. God has a plan for you.

Start thanking him for what He has done for you, and what he has seen you through. It is never too late, as long as you have breath to do what is right. If you have been walking down a road with your life and you know it is wrong or that God is calling you to go a different way, don't be afraid. If you feel that you are at the bottom, the only way to move is up. So, why not take a few steps?

If you are unsure, ask the LORD, "Am I going the right way? He will show you if you ask. Remember nothing is too small or too big for God. He created the whole universe, and every gigantic and miniscule thing in it. Whatever problem you have, ask Him. Matthew 6:27 says, "Which of you by taking thought can add one cubit unto his stature?" You can't, but you can choose to serve the God who can. Why do you worry and fret and try to fix things that are out of your control? Cast all your worries and troubles and trials on the One who can do something about it. He is waiting. Will you let him help you?

My hope, your hope, our hope is in the LORD. He will never leave you. He will go with you all the way. Trust Him.

CHAPTER TWELVE

Many things happen in our lives that we have no control over but not one time has Jesus ever left me. Everyone has a past, but not everyone has a future. Where will you spend your time? 1Corinthians 15:22 says, "For as in Adam all die, even so in Christ shall all be made alive."

We will all die. The question is, when? The question that we should have is where will we be going after we die. If you are lost and not believing in Christ, it will be the lake of fire. Revelation 21:8 says, "But the fearful, and unbelieving, and the abominable, and the murderers, and the whoremongers, and the sorcerers, and the adulterers, and all liars, shall have their part in the lake which burneth with fire and brimstone: which is the second death." If you believe in Christ and you have asked Him to come live within you, then you are saved from this place and Heaven shall be your home. Romans 6:23 says, "For the wages of sin is death; but the gift of God is eternal life through Jesus Christ our LORD." All that really matters in this world is that you know Jesus, and that your name is written in the Book of Life.

We all have a past, present, and a future. You can't do anything about your past except give it to God and ask Him if there is someone you need to forgive, or someone you need to ask to forgive you. Maybe it is someone who has hurt you. You may even be bitter about it, but you can't let it stand between you and your rewards in Heaven. When bitterness and anger stay in your heart, it takes up the space that Christ needs to live and work inside of you.

I believe this is why we see so many unhappy Christians, they have stored up all that bitterness and anger around their heart, and it shows in their actions and spews out of their mouth. I have learned to forgive without the person even asking it of me. This is not easy sometimes because the flesh and its pride want to remind my brain and my heart of how I have been wronged. But, I remind myself that Christ only uses the broken and He must have room in my heart to do that.

As I said earlier in this book, He will not force you to trust Him, and the devil will try many ways to remind you of your past. The devil is a cunning trickster and he will send people into your life to remind you of things you have done wrong. The devil will enter your dreams to make you feel or believe things that aren't true. The devil uses every opportunity he can to make sure that you never let go of your past because he knows that if you are free, God can use you to help others. The devil will cloud your mind and steal it if you let him. If you concentrate on your past, your mind and your heart have no room left to concentrate on how to help others. If your brain and your heart are full of yourself, then you are seeing yourself, not Christ. When your heart and mind are open to the LORD, He can use you by placing things in your mind such as people you need to be praying for, others in need and headed for hell, or knowing what to do to help others.

When you fill your mind with your past or even thoughts of wishing you could go back to times when things were what you thought was easier in your life, then the LORD cannot use you. When you are walking with Christ, and you start getting closer to Him your mind will be in the present and the future. You have to work to keep your mind in the present and the future. Colossians 3:1-3 says, "If ye then being risen with Christ, seek those things which are above, where Christ sitteth on the right hand of God. Set your affections on things above, not on things of this earth. For ye are dead, and your life is hid with Christ in God." This is why we, as children of God, are not to worry about the things of this earth because they will fade. But in time, we will live forever in Heaven. We are already seated there. This is why when we close our eyes here, we open them in Heaven.

The devil's job is to steal your peace and your joy, and he doesn't want you to speak of Christ and tell of all the things He has brought you through and what He has saved you from because this is your testimony. If the world hears your story bringing glory to Jesus, then they will hear of the goodness of God. The devil is a liar.

I could give you scripture, tell you to quote after me or pray a simple prayer, but the truth is you must have *faith*. You must have faith to believe that Christ is who He says He is, and He will do what He says He will do. You must believe that He came and willingly laid down his life for *you*, that you are a sinner, and only through Him living, dying, and being raised again are you saved. You must be willing to accept this gift from God.

Ephesians 2:8 says, *For by grace are you saved* (This is what God gives you: grace and salvation) *through faith*; (You must believe what He says) *and not of yourselves*: (You can't save yourself) *It is the gift of God.* Romans 10:9 says, *"If thou shall confess with your mouth the Lord Jesus, and shalt believe in thine heart that God hath raised Him from the dead, thou shalt be saved."*

Jesus is waiting and calling for you. My prayer is that you hear Him before the final trumpet sounds. If you have prayed this prayer and you have accepted His gift of salvation, call someone and tell them. And then, remember that wherever you go, God is with you.

ABOUT THE AUTHOR

Melissa Halstead is truly and totally devoted to Jesus. She has seen His hand move in her own life and wants to use every opportunity to share Him with others so that they can have a real relationship with Him. She is happily married, has two children, three grandchildren, and is living a life beyond what she could have asked or imagined because of God's sufficient grace.

ABOUT MANIFEST PUBLICATIONS

Manifest Publications is the publishing division of Manifest International, LLC. Our objective is to help like-minded ministries and writers produce and distribute materials which proclaim Jesus Christ to all the world and equip the global Church for unity and maturity.

www.manifestinternational.com